CONTENTS

CHAPTER ONE

MEET THE LABRADOODLE

Do you like dogs with shaggy fur coats and floppy ears? Then the Labradoodle may be the perfect dog for you and your family! These dogs are affectionate and energetic companions. It's no wonder that Labradoodles are one of the world's most popular dogs.

Labradoodles are a type of crossbreed dog. A crossbreed dog is a cross between two **breeds**. The breeds are usually chosen for certain traits, or qualities. A Labradoodle is a cross between a Labrador retriever and a poodle. Labradors and poodles are **purebred** dogs. Labradoodles get their traits from both breeds.

 breed a type of dog that has specific traits

purebred a dog that is the same breed as its parents

Top Crossbreed Dogs

ODLE

ievers

raintree
a Capstone company — publishers for children

Raintree is an imprint of Capstone Global Library Limited, a company incorporated in England and Wales having its registered office at 264 Banbury Road, Oxford, OX2 7DY – Registered company number: 6695582

www.raintree.co.uk
myorders@raintree.co.uk

Editor: Maddie Spalding
Designer and Production Specialist: Laura Polzin
Printed and bound in India

ISBN: 978 1 4747 6855 9
10 9 8 7 6 5 4 3 2 1
23 22 21 20 19

British Library Cataloguing in Publication Data
A full catalogue record for this book is available from the British Library.

Acknowledgements
iStockphoto: Bigandt_Photography, 20–21, Darren Brown, cover, fotografixx, 22–23, Michelle Hovet, 28–29, monkeybusinessimages, 4–5, PierceHSmith, 16–17, rbulthuis, 24–25, Steve Debenport, 26–27; Newscom: Atkison Helen/SIPA, 9, LWA/Sharie Kennedy Blend Images, 11; Shutterstock Images: Bigandt.com, 18, Hollysdogs, 14–15, Jeanne Provost, 12–13, KariDesign, 26, Saranellieart, 19, The Dog Photographer, 6–7.
Design elements: bittbox.

Every effort has been made to contact copyright holders of material reproduced in this book. Any omissions will be rectified in subsequent printings if notice is given to the publisher.

All the internet addresses (URLs) given in this book were valid at the time of going to press. However, due to the dynamic nature of the internet, some addresses may have changed, or sites may have changed or ceased to exist since publication. While the author and publisher regret any inconvenience this may cause readers, no responsibility for any such changes can be accepted by either the author or the publisher.

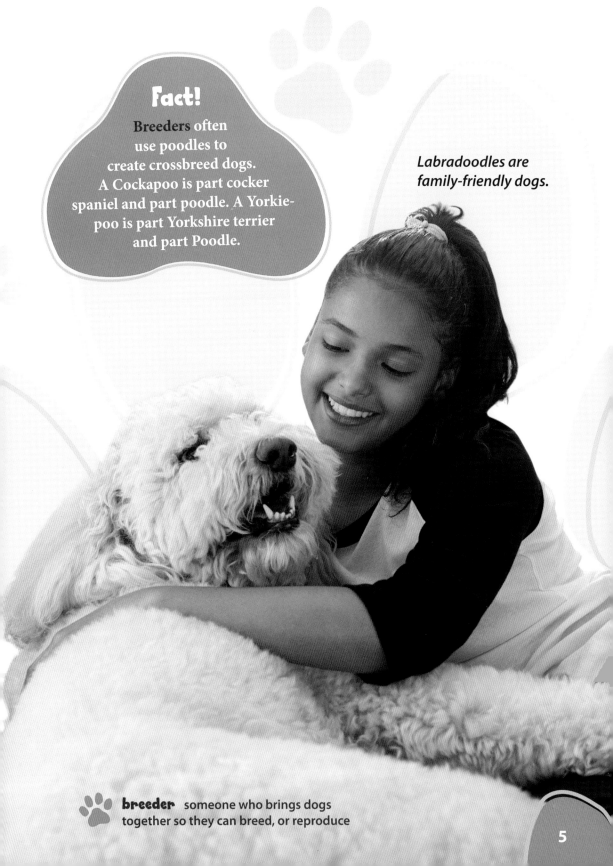

Fact!

Breeders often use poodles to create crossbreed dogs. A Cockapoo is part cocker spaniel and part poodle. A Yorkie-poo is part Yorkshire terrier and part Poodle.

Labradoodles are family-friendly dogs.

breeder someone who brings dogs together so they can breed, or reproduce

The Australian Labradoodle

In the UK, breeders sell Labradoodles that have poodle and labrador retriever parents. These Labradoodle puppies can each have very different traits. For this reason, the UK Labradoodle is not a breed. To be a breed, the dogs each have to have the same traits. In Australia, people breed Labradoodles with other Labradoodles to try to create a Labradoodle breed.

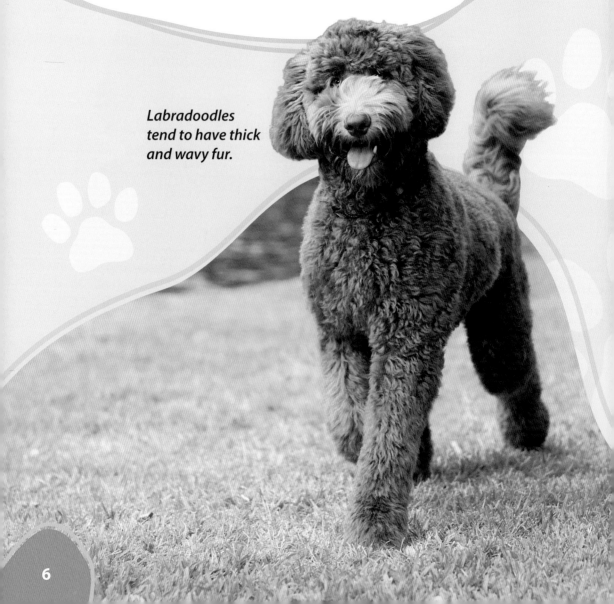

Labradoodles tend to have thick and wavy fur.

WHY CHOOSE A LABRADOODLE?

People choose Labradoodles for many reasons. Some people who have dog allergies choose Labradoodles. People with dog allergies react to a dog's saliva and dander. Dander is tiny flakes of dry skin. People with dog allergies may react to dander after they pet a dog. Their skin may get itchy. They may get watery eyes. Some people may have trouble breathing. Poodles and some other breeds shed less fur than other types of dogs. Dogs that shed less fur produce less dander. Some Labradoodles get this trait from poodles. These dogs are less likely to bother someone who is allergic to dogs.

Purebred dogs can have health problems. Some people choose crossbreed dogs because they believe these dogs are less likely to have such health problems. Whatever your reason for choosing the Labradoodle, there's a lot to love about this adorable dog.

CHAPTER TWO

LABRADOODLE HISTORY

In 1988, a woman called Pat Blum needed a **guide dog**. She had limited vision. Blum and her husband lived in Hawaii. Her husband was allergic to every breed of guide dog available in Hawaii. Blum had to search outside Hawaii to find a guide dog. But she would have trouble bringing a dog from somewhere else into the state. No animal in Hawaii has ever had rabies. This virus can be deadly to dogs and humans. There are rules to keep the virus out of Hawaii. If a dog comes from a place where rabies has been found, such as the rest of the United States, the dog must be put into **quarantine**. Blum did not want her dog to have to be in quarantine.

 guide dog a dog that helps people with vision problems to move around safely

quarantine a place where an animal is kept alone until proven healthy so it doesn't spread disease

Some Labradoodles are service dogs.

Pat Blum learned that dogs from Australia can come into Hawaii without having to be quarantined. This is because the rabies virus hasn't spread to Australia. Blum contacted the Royal Guide Dog Association of Australia. This group bred and trained guide dogs. Blum hoped the association could help her find a guide dog that wouldn't trigger her husband's allergies.

BREEDING A NEW DOG

Wally Conron was the association's puppy breeding manager. People contacted him whenever they needed a guide dog. Conron went to work to find Blum a dog. He knew that a standard poodle would be big enough to serve as a guide dog. He also thought a poodle would be perfect because not many people are allergic to poodles. Conron took fur and saliva samples from 33 different standard poodles. He sent the samples to Mr Blum's doctors. All of the samples triggered his allergies, so none of the poodles would work.

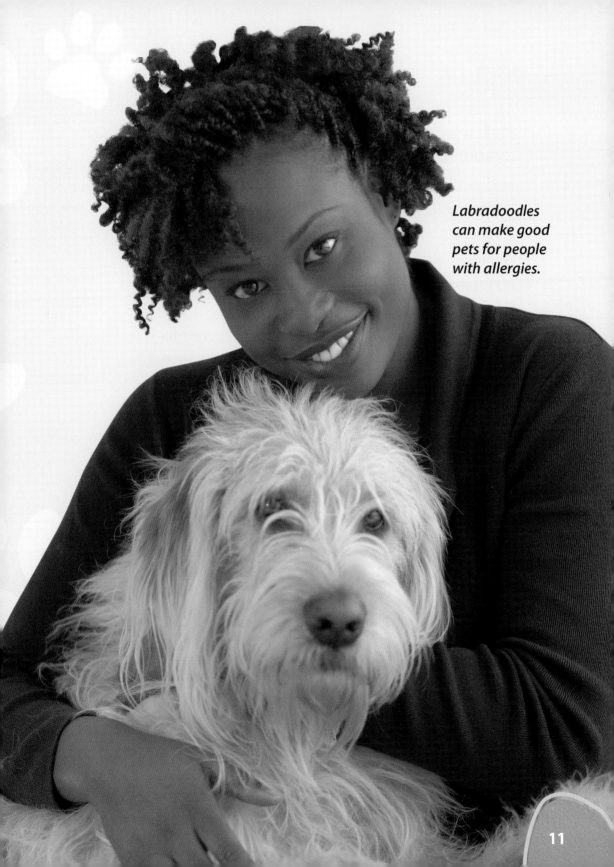

Labradoodles can make good pets for people with allergies.

Conron didn't give up. He knew that labrador retrievers are clever and easily trained. So he decided to try crossing a labrador retriever with a standard poodle. Three puppies were born. Conron again sent fur and saliva samples to Hawaii. Mr. Blum reacted to two of the puppies but not to the third. A possible guide dog had been found. Conron named this puppy Sultan.

Fact !

Wally Conron bred 31 Labradoodle puppies in total. Today he has a labrador retriever. He has never had his own pet Labradoodle.

A female Labradoodle usually gives birth to six to eight puppies at a time.

Sultan worked well for the Blums. Conron hoped this type of dog could help other people too. He bred another **litter**. Ten puppies were born. Only three were low allergy. Conron had hoped more of the dogs would be low allergy.

Sultan was soon in the news. People became excited about this new dog breed. The Labradoodle's intelligence and friendly personality made it popular. People started breeding Labradoodles in the UK. Today, Labradoodles are bred as family-friendly pets. Some are also bred to be therapy dogs. Therapy dogs help comfort people who are sick or who have disabilities.

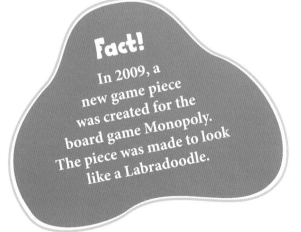

Fact!
In 2009, a new game piece was created for the board game Monopoly. The piece was made to look like a Labradoodle.

 litter a group of puppies born from the same mother

CHAPTER THREE

ALL ABOUT THE LABRADOODLE

Labradoodles are friendly dogs. They seem happy and excited when they are around people. It isn't just their owners they appear to adore. Many of them are friendly towards everyone they meet.

Labradoodles enjoy playing. But their high level of energy can sometimes be a problem. A playful Labradoodle can jump up on people when it gets excited. Luckily Labradoodles are often easy to train.

Labradoodles are clever and curious dogs.

Labradoodle heroes

Labradoodles are known for their intelligence. This trait has helped them save people's lives. Two Labradoodles came to a stranger's rescue in January 2018. It was early morning in a small town in Michigan, USA. The dogs barked until they woke their owners, Lonnie and Susan Chester. One of the dogs tugged on Lonnie's sleeve until the man got out of bed. He followed the dogs to the door. The dogs ran outside when Lonnie opened the door. The dogs led Lonnie to a woman who was lying on the Chesters' driveway. Lonnie carried the woman inside. He knew she needed help. He called the police. It was −13 degrees Celsius (9 degrees Fahrenheit) outside. Without the help of the two dogs, the woman could have died.

BIG AND SMALL

Labradoodles come in three different sizes. This is because their poodle parents can vary in size. Standard Labradoodles are usually 53 to 61 centimetres (21 to 24 inches) tall. Height is measured to the top of a dog's shoulder. The weight of a standard Labradoodle can vary from 23 to 29 kilograms (50 to 65 pounds).

Medium Labradoodles are typically 43 to 51 centimetres (17 to 20 inches) tall. They often weigh between 14 and 20 kilograms (30 and 45 pounds).

Miniature Labradoodles are usually 36 to 41 centimetres (14 to 16 inches) tall. Their weight can vary from 7 to 11 kilograms (15 to 25 pounds).

Labradoodles are small when they are puppies, but they get bigger quickly.

COATS AND COLOURS

Labradoodles can also vary in coat colour and **texture**. Some have soft and silky coats. Their fur is wavy or curly. This type of coat is called a fleece coat. Other Labradoodles have a coat that feels like a lamb's wool. This type of coat is called a wool coat. A Labradoodle with a wool coat will have curlier fur than a dog with a fleece coat.

Some Labradoodles have thicker or shaggier coats than others.

texture   the feel of something, such as a dog's fur

Another Labradoodle coat type is called the hair coat. Fur in a hair coat is straight or slightly wavy. A hair coat isn't as silky as a fleece coat. Labradoodles with a hair coat tend to shed a lot. They are the most likely of the Labradoodle types to cause allergies.

Labradoodles come in many different colours. A Labradoodle's coat might be black, yellow or brown. Other Labradoodle coat colours include cream, red, silver or white. A Labradoodle's coat can also be more than one colour.

Some Labradoodles have coats with patches of different colours.

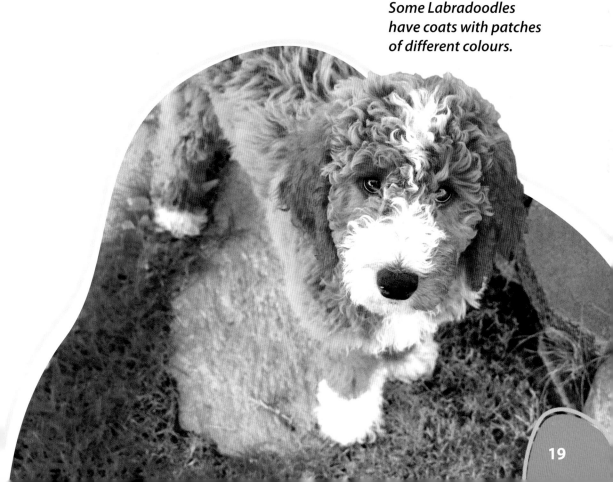

CHAPTER FOUR

CARING FOR YOUR LABRADOODLE

Before deciding to get a Labradoodle, your family should think about what it will need. All dogs should be **groomed**. Grooming includes brushing and combing your dog's coat. Brushing cleans the dog's coat. Combing keeps it free of tangles.

Some Labradoodles have shorter coats that do not tangle. Owners can groom these types of Labradoodles at home. Other Labradoodles have longer fleece or wool coats. Special equipment is needed to groom these types of coats. People who own these types of Labradoodles should take their dogs to a professional groomer about once every four to six weeks.

 groom care for a dog's coat

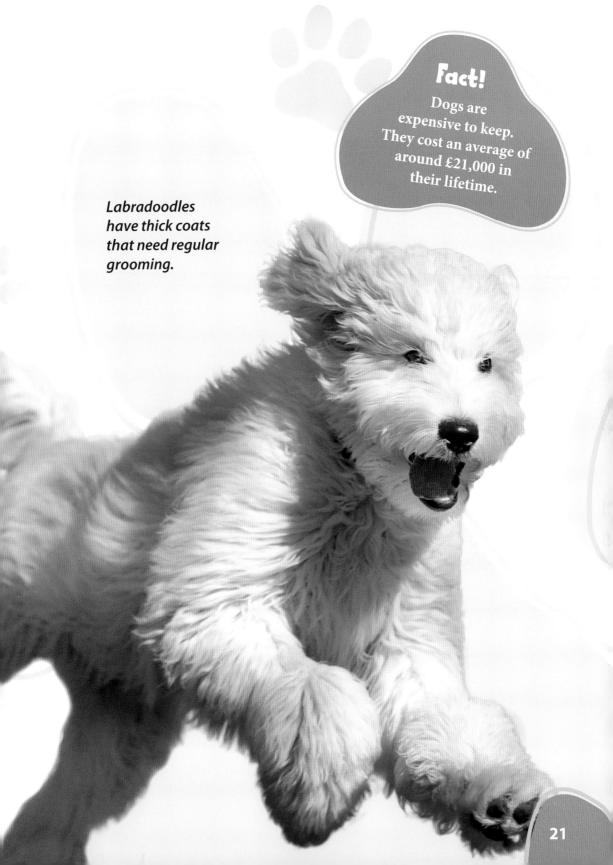

Labradoodles have thick coats that need regular grooming.

Fact!
Dogs are expensive to keep. They cost an average of around £21,000 in their lifetime.

DIET AND EXERCISE

Like all dogs, Labradoodles need exercise and a healthy diet. Most Labradoodles need 30 to 60 minutes of exercise each day. Your vet can recommend the best type of food for your dog. Most Labradoodles eat one to two-and-a-half cups of food per day. The amount varies depending on your dog's size. You should split the food into two meals each day.

It is also important to socialize your Labradoodle. Socializing involves having your dog spend time with people and other dogs. You can arrange play times for your dog with other dogs. The other dogs should be dogs of a similar size and energy level to your Labradoodle. These types of dogs will be most likely to get along well with your Labradoodle. Socializing your Labradoodle will help it learn how to behave well around other dogs.

Fact!

Some Labradoodles are good at dock diving. Dock diving is a competition in which a person throws an object from a dock into water. The dog that jumps the farthest wins!

*Labradoodles love
to run and play.*

When Labradoodles swim, moisture can become trapped in their ears and cause infection.

LABRADOODLE HEALTH

Both poodles and Labrador retrievers tend to develop hip dysplasia. Labradoodles could **inherit** this condition. In hip dysplasia, the upper leg bone does not fit snugly into the hip joint. Labradoodles can also develop elbow dysplasia. This condition usually occurs when a dog's elbow bones do not grow properly. It causes swelling and joint pain in a dog's elbow. Dysplasia is painful. Dogs who have dysplasia will often develop a limp.

Another health problem that Labradoodles can develop is progressive retinal atrophy (PRA). The retina is a part of the eye. It receives images and sends signals to the brain so the brain can identify images. PRA damages the retina over time. A dog with PRA will lose some or all of its vision.

Labradoodles can get ear **infections**. Ear infections can happen when moisture gets inside a dog's ears. Then germs can get into the ear. Ear infections cause ear pain and difficulty hearing. A Labradoodle's floppy ears easily trap moisture, especially when it swims. After a swim, dry your dog's ears carefully. Check your dog's ears at least once a week for signs of infection, such as redness or a bad smell.

inherit get a trait from a parent or ancestor

infection a condition that occurs when germs such as bacteria and viruses get inside the body of a person or animal

Vets can usually treat these health issues with medicine or surgery. Sometimes a special diet and exercise help these problems get better. You should take your Labradoodle to the vet at least once a year for a check-up. Your vet will also give your Labradoodle regular **vaccinations**. These vaccinations help protect your Labradoodle against diseases.

 vaccination a shot of a medicine that prevents a person or animal from getting a disease

Your family should also talk to your vet about having your Labradoodle neutered or spayed. Neutering involves removing a part of a male animal's body that helps it make babies. Spaying is a similar process, but it is done for a female animal. These operations can keep your dog from having puppies. Dogs that aren't spayed or neutered can have many puppies. It can be hard for one family to take care of or find a home for many puppies.

Regular visits to the vet can help keep your Labradoodle healthy.

CHOOSING A LABRADOODLE

If your family is ready to get a Labradoodle, searching for a licensed breeder is a good place to start. Your family should ask the breeder whether the dog has been to a vet and received all of the vaccinations it needs. The breeder should give you the vet's records.

The breeder should also give you information about the Labradoodle's family history. This will help you find out if any health conditions run in the dog's family. Your family could also try finding a Labradoodle at a rescue centre or dog shelter. People at the centre or shelter may have information about the dog's background.

Having a pet is a big responsibility. But it is also a lot of fun. If you like to get outside and go walking, the Labradoodle may be the perfect dog for you and your family.

Labradoodles are beloved members of many families.

GLOSSARY

breed a type of dog that has specific traits

breeder someone who brings dogs together so they can breed, or reproduce

groom to care for a dog's coat

guide dog a dog that helps people with vision problems move around safely

infection a condition that occurs when germs such as bacteria and viruses get inside the body of a person or animal

inherit get a trait from a parent or ancestor

litter a group of puppies born from the same mother

purebred a dog that is the same breed as its parents

quarantine a place where an animal is kept alone until proven healthy so it doesn't spread disease

texture the feel of something, such as a dog's fur

vaccination a shot of a medicine that prevents a person or animal from getting a disease

FIND OUT MORE

BOOKS

Dogs (Animal Family Albums), Paul Mason (Raintree, 2013)

The Dog Encyclopedia for Kids, Tammy Gagne (Raintree, 2017)

The Truth about Dogs: What Dogs Do When You're Not Looking (Pets Undercover!), Mary Colson (Raintree, 2017)

WEBSITES

The Labradoodle Association of the UK website has plenty of information about Labradoodles:
www.labradoodle.org.uk

Find out lots of fun Labradoodle facts, including breed characteristics, personality and its history:
dogtime.com/dog-breeds/labradoodle

INDEX